Cracking Your
DNA

Cracking Your

DNA

DISTINCT | NATURAL | ABILITIES

WADDIE WALTON

Library of Congress Control Number: 2017900853
ISBN: Hardcover   978-1-5245-7695-0
                   Softcover   978-1-5245-7696-7
                   eBook   978-1-5245-7697-4

Print information available on the last page.

Rev. date: 01/27/2017

To order additional copies of this book, contact:
Xlibris
1-888-795-4274
www.Xlibris.com
Orders@Xlibris.com
753295

Contents

I would like to begin by stating that this is a short book intended for those who are searching for a purpose-driven read; those who seek advice from a person that can sum it up in less than a day of reading. Cracking Your DNA will enlighten you on how to start out and engage with people who can motivate and direct you toward cracking your DNA, which stands for distinct, natural, ability, in order to profit from your innate talents. It is my hope that through this writing I am able to touch individuals who are interested in learning more about their natural self. This book was designed to better equip people with the tools to tap into their second-nature abilities. After discovering such abilities, I will provide Words from Waddie, also known as tips, on how to become an entrepreneur and capitalize off of your distinct, natural, abilities. The marketing tool that I will employ is social media, which has proven itself to be very effective and lucrative. Now let's begin the journey to cracking your DNA!

About Waddie Ann Walton
(or Welcome to Waddie's World)

I am a single mother of three children; two daughters, Kiandra and Nieya, and one son, Zarrion. Though I'm the middle child, I don't suffer from middle child syndrome. I proudly hold a Master's degree in Organizational leadership, an accomplishment that helped to fuel this book. During the course of my college career I was provided the elements that defined my interests and aspirations of owning myself and tapping into my DNA. But, I have a confession to make: For years, I didn't feel that I would gain my wealth through obtaining higher education. I felt that my DNA, talents, and strong entrepreneurial spirit would gain me the weight and success I needed to live a financially fruitful life. I'm not advising anyone to neglect their goal of obtaining higher education; it's a sense of self accomplishment that paves the path for professional growth and building your company's success. I have also experienced that the alphabet behind your name awards respect and recognition in professional and social settings. A degree states that you took the time to educate yourself beyond societal standards, which is worthy to be rewarded through a higher salary, mobility within your organization or distinction in a professional biography for *your* business.

I have two brothers who were both born with muscular dystrophy, which is a destabilizing disease. I have the utmost respect for their strength and determination to not let their inability to walk define their purpose. Furthermore, I developed an even greater admiration for my mother who cared for them their entire lives without giving up on them. This is one of many characteristics that she has instilled in me about mother hood.

I'm a southern girl by birth, however my family moved to the Midwest when I was nine years old, and then into the Chicago Housing Authorities projects! These projects were also known as Robert Taylor Homes, which were a very different environment from my roots in the South. From the way I spoke and dressed to the food I ate and the school system I was accustomed to, I had to learn to adjust to a place where I simply did not fit. We went from living in a small town home with my grandparents to being thrown into the big city, which was mostly a dangerous ghetto, affectionally known as the 'hood. I went from fresh vegetable gardens, a rural and a spacious area to run and play in the hot streets of Arkansas to extreme, seemingly unbearable weather conditions in Illinois. In 1979 Chicago, one day could be sweltering and the next day could be brutally cold, not to mention this was the first time I'd ever seen snow in person. That same year, Illinois was recorded to have witnessed the coldest winter of its time. We moved onto the seventh floor, the highest that I had ever been in my life. I had never been on an elevator nor a stair well, the smell of urine permeated the entire floor, and little people like me were using words that even my parents did not say. But I never conformed to this lifestyle. We lived there for 10 years, which allowed me to foster life-long relationships with some of my dearest friends. Those same friends have been my biggest support in life. I also met classmates who would encourage and inspire me to embrace my DNA. The memories from the projects range from hope and happiness to sometimes sad and deadly.

It was in Chicago, at age 14, that I recall attending my second funeral for a classmate who had been murdered. Before that I had only attended my grandmother's funeral, which frightened the hell out of me! I was seven years old and associated death with creepy, frightful images that television had created. But as my life continued in the projects, I would go on to attend funerals for classmates or other peers. Unfortunately, such casualties became normal for my friends and I. This was only one of several dilemmas that we faced while growing up as black children drenched in an impoverished neighborhood. I went on to graduate from high school and attempted to attend community college, but by this time we had migrated to the North Side of Chicago. The North Side of Chicago was even more overwhelming than transitioning from the South to the Midwest. I was delighted to indulge in the variety of foods, lifestyle, etc., and it was even more refreshing than anything I had ever experienced. Although I attempted to pursue a college degree, I soon dropped out after I had become pregnant with my first child. This situation caused me to become extremely depressed and lonely, especially after I lost him due to a premature delivery. After the death of my baby I had gone into a deep abyss. Because I was in a dark place in life, I eventually built relationships with some toxic people, especially the 'bad boys' and shady friends. Details on that lifestyle will be featured in the next book! But, I must say, running with the wrong crowd birthed an unexpected silver lining that would change my life indefinitely.

About six years into my new, rogue set of friends, God planted a blessing in the form of a child into my womb. My daughter, who has an abundance of red hair (my little red head) changed my entire world and outlook on life. It is she who gave me priorities and a new perspective on everything that I had faced up until that point. Tears of joy streamed down my face as the doctors placed her into my arms.

Soon after her arrival I began to prioritize my life and enrolled into cosmetology school, which allowed me to earn my cosmetology license. The license afforded me the opportunity to work in a salon and hopefully gain a substantial clientele so that I could leave my mother's house. However, it was not that simple and I was not that patient, so I averted my passion in hair for a career in corporate America. But, my eagerness to own myself was tested when I would meet several women who encouraged me toward the path of entrepreneurship. Such encouragement empowered me to pursue higher education and build wealthy relationships with people who could help me on my journey to owning myself.

I first met Emily Swain, an older co-worker who served as a mentor, at Fresenius Medical Center. She taught me about the rigorous process of becoming a property investor and mentored me as I shifted my crowd of friends. With her help I learned how to interact with millionaires while simultaneously learning how they earned their millions. In result of her mentorship my mother and I became millionaire property investors in a very short time. This was my first business venture that I shared with my business partner, mommy.

I went on to meet Joy Holly, whom I admired for her physical beauty and equally inner beautiful characteristics. I respected the way she permitted her naturally youthful, energetic and genuine personality traits to yield her success as a savvy professional, wife and mother. Then came my sister, Jessie Adams, who inspired me to further my education and pursue a Master's degree. To this day she is the most intelligent and supportive sister that I have in my circle. Next would have to be my lifelong soul sister, Tessa Lorraine, who has my heart in her hand thanks to her benevolent spirit. Lastly, my good girl-friend, Elaine Gillespie, who is responsible for teaching me the rules of motherhood, friendship and respect. She did this willingly and was also there to enlighten me when I was unreasonable. Her greatest gift to our friendship is that of accountability; she tells me when I am plain wrong and corrects me with compassion. Each of these women have impacted my life tremendously and I am deeply grateful for their friendship.

Words from Waddie

O **WfW**: *We need a support system in order to become successful at anything, be it professional or personal. The dynamic women that I mentioned have served as an irreplaceable support system. As I continue to allow the Lord to improve my life, I realize that I am a better woman than I was yesterday because of my sister-friends. My goal is to impact and motivate those who share my vision of owning themselves. It will take patience, which is a skill that I prayed for throughout my path to greatness. I am grateful that my God allows others to open their ears in hopes of receiving gifts from family, friends, co-workers or even me!*

O **WfW**: *Always be willing to learn from the smallest person in the room. I believe that if your brain isn't sucking in some type of useful information, despite who the information is coming from, then it is not being used to the best of its ability. This notion has taught me to constantly think of techniques to build my brand and move upward toward my imagination's pinnacle of success.*

O **WfW**: *Don't be a Gold Digger but a* **Goal Digger***, set seemingly unreachable goals for yourself and continue to progress toward that once feared level of success. These helps to increase your brain power. Setting small goals for small achievements will help you to practice setting bigger goals for a magnum of success.*

Some unfavorable characteristics of an entrepreneur are tendencies of OCD (Obsessive-Compulsive Disorder) or ADHD (Attention Deficit Hyperactivity Disorder). Trust your instinct and create from your gut feeling.

Not a Product of My Environment

Where do I begin? I am not a product of my environment, but a product of the two people who created me. First, I'll introduce my mother, to whom I credit my creative personality. Secondly, I credit my father for his part in helping to create me, although I never had the opportunity to know him. After learning of his death I googled him, only to find bits and pieces about he, his family and family's business. It's important to know those from whom you come, especially as it relates to cracking to your DNA. For years I had so many unanswered questions about myself, more specifically I wondered where I gained my strong sense of self, intrinsic self-motivation and business-like mentality. Where did I get my strong sense of entrepreneurship? I had all of these questions but did not have anyone to directly answer, as my mother wasn't forth coming with such personal information about my father. In fact, she hardly mentioned his name to me. After listening to lots of small talk about his family, I was finally able to form some memories. His life was like the family's secret that no one wants to address. My family acted as though they were sworn to secrecy when it came to acknowledging my father. I perceived it as if my brother and I were a product of shame.

But, his absence never defined my purpose for existing, actually, I lived a fairly simple and care-free life as a child. My mother filled both conscious and subconscious voids as it related to my father's absence. I thoroughly connected with the old adage, "You can't miss something that you never had". I never envied my siblings who had their fathers in the lives. My mother described me as an adorable, wide-eyed young girl who sat quietly at church, unaware of the drama that surrounded her little world. Although this book won't go into detail about that chapter of my life, it would make for an intense, suspenseful read that would give Tyler Perry's "Have and Have Nots" a run for its money!

Nevertheless, the meat of cracking your DNA is about discovering the three wonders of your world, which include the why, who, and when certain events happened in your life. Once you have unlocked these key elements you will become informed on aspects of your life that you may have underestimated. Since my father was a complete mystery, there were some parts of my DNA that seemed inevitable locked. Thankfully my mother was an awesome role model and amazing woman. She dedicated her life to equipping my siblings and I with quality life values and character traits. To date mother has been my greatest supporter and I am thrilled to call her my BFF!

After processing such life-experiences, I was determined to buckle down and commit to writing a self-reflective book that would empower, motivate and coach others who are searching to own themselves. I have learned that the only way to successfully brand myself is fully own myself. This success isn't measured by someone else's assessment of your life, but by your standard of success. You are solely responsible for your work ethic, the time and sacrifices that you make in efforts of achieving your dreams. The question that you have to ask yourself is, what would take you to that next level of achievement? I'll share some of my personal business experiences that will inspire you to remain steadfast and faithful to your dreams of owning yourself.

Entrepreneurship is about solving problems, thus, most entrepreneurs are obsessed with thinking of creative, innovative method to solve problems. This may cause some people to prematurely diagnose us with OCD, ADHD, and other forms of mental disorders. In reality, we are esteemed individuals who are not afraid of the grind and hustle that it takes to make it to the top! I can recall the days that I sat at my eight-hour, hourly wage job day-dreaming about my next venture. I offer this piece of advice when cracking your DNA at your day job: in order to see your dreams come into fruition you have to sleep it, eat it, speak it and most importantly, **believe** it! In my family I'm known as the outspoken, over the top fashionista who takes risk with faith in the Creator. Some business owners say that one should not give their time, advice or product for free, however, I totally disagree with that notion since I am giver by nature. My passion for humanitarianism can sometime be overwhelming, but the feeling of helping people achieve their goals is incomparable.

Experience has been my best teacher, both good and bad experiences have shaped my business life. It was after losing my long-time, "good job" that God granted me the opportunity to own my very first business. It was my severance package that funded my dreams of opening a hair salon. Sadly, I was only in business for a meager two years. A few words to sum up my life during that time would be failure, struggle and sacrifice. I lost everything; my car was repossessed, house went into foreclosure and I was sued by the mortgage company and the auto-finance company. I was then forced into bankruptcy, only to realize that my previous employer didn't release enough funds to cover my home. Though this was a devastating reality, I now know how it feels to forfeit everything to reach my goals. Such an experience caused me to grieve and question my definition of success. As the sole provider for my family and my children's personal super hero, it was important that I exhibited all phases of success, showing them that sometimes success does not pay in finance, but more so in personal achievement.

It was my 48th birthday and my youngest daughter, who was now employed, purchased a gift for me for the first time. She spared no expense as she bought me a gift from my favorite store, which was quite pricy for her wallet. After presenting me with the gift, she treated me to dinner and surprised me with balloons and a sentimental card that made my heart melt. The words that she wrote in the card were by far the cherry on the pie for me. Her words proved that I had achieved my personal goal of being an awesome role model, considering I was a single mother of three. The words read, "Every mother deserves special recognition on her birthday if you were not my mom already I'll be jealous of whoever was your daughter. You're such an inspiring and motivating mom. Love, Nieya!" Those loving words were all the comfort that I needed during my time of despair.

As badly as I would have liked them to, those words did not erase the debt that I had incurred as a business owner. Another word from Waddie: failure is a good thing, it's what you do with the experiences behind your failures that make you a winner! I learned so much about myself in owning my own business. I learned that I didn't like to manage people and that I was better suited in customer service so that I can utilize my people skills. I was known as the hostess with the mostest in my salon! I greeted all the clients with a warm and welcoming smile, provided a relaxing, tranquil environment and ensured them that they would receive excellent service. I learned my weaknesses and my strengths and used them to elevate me in my process of owning myself. I didn't know it at the time, but God was preparing a greater plan for my life. Upon the closure of my salon, I had the daunting task of informing my staff that we would no longer be in business. It was received well by one of the stylist who had been there for a short time. She voiced her opinion and expressed that she didn't want to leave because it was an ideal location to grow a steady clientele. I explained to her that this could be an opportunity for her to establish her own salon. I provided her with the leasing manager's contact information so that she could inquire about taking over the lease. She was grateful that I shared the information with her and showed interest in her personal growth as a stylist. This instance compares to my regard for mentorship and sharing pertinent information that is valuable to another person. To her, such new knowledge was worth more than tangible money. This experience also taught me the advantage of building relationships with people who share the same vision of owning themselves. This way, everyone wins!

Cracking your DNA is similar to unlocking your purpose on earth. Some go an entire life time without unleashing their purpose or fulfilling their God given mission. To unveil your DNA and help others to the same is an extraordinary feat. By leading my former employee into the direction of entrepreneurship, I was assisting her in expediting a goal that she did not think would happen in the near future. Though she was afraid initially, I encouraged her to accept the new journey. There were a plethora of topics that I covered in order to prepare for the new challenge. I assured her that she would reach some success, but there would also be pitfalls that would discourage her from maintaining business. As our bond strengthened, I informed her that as a sole proprietor she would have to conduct extensive research on how to save money because amenities such as a monetary safety net, 401K, paid time off, health insurance or retirement fund are not provided by anyone. Because I have a corporate background, I advised her to consult with a financial adviser. Although this particular business didn't work well for me, I exclaimed my happiness for her new endeavor. I processed the overhead cost so that she knew I was genuinely invested in her new enterprise. After this chapter of my life had officially concluded, I established my newest and most passionate brainchild, Sassy Girl Sandwich & So.

Sassy Girl Sandwich & So. is an online sandwich company that delivers sandwiches and other baked goods, as well as a myriad of crafty, specialty items. My new company was the nudge that I needed to tap into my DNA. It is a creative outlet that I employ to create customized gift baskets, personalized ornaments, t-shirts, glassware and other miscellaneous crafts. My creations ignite joy in the hearts of my customers. With a profit margin of more thirty-three percent, I am exited and grateful to officially launch Sassy Girl Sandwich & So. both locally and nationally. My clientele has increased dramatically thanks to the globalized attention from social media marketing. Social media has enabled business owners to reach an audience that would otherwise be unavailable. Apps like Instagram, Twitter and Facebook have allotted free marketing and promotion tools that are extremely lucrative.

Words from Waddie

O *WfW: Survey your product or service through social media outlets for FREE! Opportunities are boundless for an entrepreneur who wishes to expand their brand globally. The virtual networking that is available will help you to purchase services with a wide network of people at very reasonable prices.*

○ *WfW: The big trend now is live feeds; this is another business tool that can sharpen public speaking skills, similar to webinars.*

○ *WfW: Take it, it's FREE! Anything you desire in life is attainable, it's only a matter of diligently working toward it! I refuse to be mediocre or stagnant in my trek to success!*

○ *WfW: Surround yourself around those who have common goals; those who motivate and remind you that failure is inevitable. But it's a temporary circumstance that only you control. Allow your failures fuel your next success! Let your intrinsic light shine through your products or service. Without an entrepreneur there wouldn't be a world!*

This sole intent of this book is to enlighten you on how to magnify your DNA and profit from such talents. God blesses all of us, even **YOU**, with distinct natural abilities. We all know someone who is innately great at something; they may not have been technically/formally trained or possess a license or certificate in a trade, but their distinct skill and polished work ethic sets them apart from anyone else. That's because God specifically ingrained that DNA into their bodies. I have discovered so much about myself, unlocked attributes that I had not recognized until I was placed in adversity and have become clear on my purpose on earth. However, cracking your DNA is time consuming and cannot be completed in one sitting. The reward that one will reap after cracking their DNA is invaluable. Cracking my DNA also combated my feelings of failure, for example, my salon was not conducive for me, but it is indeed a blessing my former employee, and her business is doing GREAT!

Create your own experience, whether it is good or bad, because at the end of the day you will have to account for your actions in life. I recall my mother attempting to save me from pitfalls by sheltering me from life's reality. She warned me that pain comes with hurt. Now that I have children, I understand exactly how she feels. As a mother my responsibility to my children is to prepare them for the real world, teach them to respect themselves, how to be responsible adults, abide by the law, pay their taxes and worship the religion of their choice. I'm not here to dictate their lives for them, that is their God-given right. Often times I think parents try way too hard to lead and direct our children once they become adults. Of course we should redirect them when they are headed toward a path of destruction, but we should not *order* their steps.

O **WfW:** *Guide, but don't force your child!*

Financially Free

I didn't want to be debt free, but free to explore my creativity. I'm also a social butterfly, so I meet friends in every setting. Another woman that has impacted my life is Dr. Susan Hood. Dr. Hood and I I met while my children were having dental work done, and she was very impressed that I owned a salon. I was surprised that someone was actually intrigued by me! We developed a fruitful friendship and would accompany one another at various entrepreneurial events. Using Facebook Live, I began promoting my other services and Dr. Hood would persuade me to suggest helpful tools that could aid other small businesses. She was most interested in the creativity that was portrayed on my website. Facebook Live allotted me the opportunity to provide valuable, FREE content that would make the owner confident in selling their products.

○ *WfW: Use the "share" approach in lieu of the "sell" approach! No one likes a salesperson, but people will listen if you are supplying them with a product or service that they are passionate about. Confidence is key, success comes after believing in yourself.*

O **Experience**: *I recently took a class on how to make candy apples with the person I had been following on social media. When she offered an online class on how to perfect that craft, I invested in myself buy purchasing a seat in her virtual classroom. She sent the materials, an instruction sheet and all of the necessary information to get into her online class. Once enrolled, I was taken shocked and appalled at her rudeness and disrespectful mannerisms in her class. Because of her age, I excused it, but I know that this is not a manner in which I would conduct my class.*

O **WFW:** *Never get too "big-headed" with the people who support you. Always be aware that someone else is offering your same service or product and you are replaceable. This woman was in tune with her DNA, but she was not a good teacher.*

O **Experience**: *Customer service is just as important as being in tuned with your DNA. She was another sister who was aware of her purpose, but did not present them pleasantly, in fact, I am surprised that she's gotten this far with her attitude. A great product should always be completed with great customer service.*

O **WfW**: *A person will forget what you said or did, but they will never forgive how you made them feel. There are a slew of social groups that offer diverse, supportive networking groups. If you don't have a friend, spouse, or family member, then share* *your vision or aspirations for entrepreneurship with someone in a virtual social circle. My greatest influences have come from strangers; remember strangers are only friends who we haven't met yet! I recently created a Facebook networking group that engages woman who share a common interest in becoming business owners but may not know how to achieve that goal. I introduced women who offer motivation, coaching, diversity and inclusion into the world of entrepreneurship. Though I have not followed through with physically meeting the members, I strive to keep in contact via social media. I have met some awesome women through these groups and I encourage you to go to networking events and vending parties. This is the gateway to becoming connected to potential opportunities that will grow your brand.*

O ***WfW****: Model the way (lead by example) and always be open to learning more techniques; these tips are great business practice to help you crack you DNA.*

O ***WfW****: Become more organic with your approach to marketing to your target audience. Be inclined to selling on small scales, never lose a client because you are not willing to go that extra mile. This is a part of creating new avenues to increase your income.*

O ***WfW****: Once, I attempted to order a product from someone to incorporate in my basket and she said that she only sells them in quantities of six. I didn't need six so I declined her service and trained myself to make the items that I needed. I was so successful that I took it as a sign from God. This sign was that I should* *stop reaching out to others who have similar DNA to me, instead I should create my own products so that it the basket is more authentic. Coupled with focus, if I work hard at a task, eventually I'll get the hang of it. Since creating my own products, I have experienced better results while also cutting an overhead cost from a third party.*

○ *WfW: Always support small businesses. Supporting the small companies will put the dollar back into the company as well as build buying power for people who look like you.*

○ *WfW: Help someone else climb the success ladder. I enjoy seeing people on social media help all of the young, or up and coming entrepreneurs market and build their brand. I try to support as many as my little dollar will allow me to. I'm not a well known motivational speaker, however, I am an expert in sharing my life lessons in hopes of teaching one how to fiscally benefit from their DNA. If this book resonates with you, then you are ready to unleash your DNA!*

○ *WfW: If you are a person of color, open a business account with a black owned bank. Taking out a business loan is also a great start to creating a fruitful business. This increases our buying power, along with shopping with other small businesses. It reflects that we are a race of people who are not divided and that we can unite our finances to thrive in this economy. Black people are surpassing any other racial group when it comes to spending and we are at the bottom of the totem poll in terms of economic prowess. If we are going to buy, we should support one another to changes those numbers.*

○ **WfW**: *Referrals are a bonus and a reward to small businesses. Offering a customer reward card will help to retain clients. It is rewarding when a new client or familiar face walks through our doors or visits our website, that is good traffic. It is even more rewarding when one refers a friend to the business via social media and in turn that friend makes a purchase!*

○ **WfW**: *Navigating your DNA to unveil your creative gifts will benefit you in the long run. Mapping out your vision is one of the first segments of manifesting your goals. Don't over think the process because if you will more than likely end up thinking yourself right out moving forward.*

○ **WfW**: *Les Brown quotes,"You can fail right into success." Please ponder this statement. An aspiring entrepreneur asked if she should take the leap of faith by launching her business. I instantly told her to dive directly into her dreams. If you think about all the pitfalls, you will spend your entire life with a burning desire to act on something that's a part of your DNA. Without entrepreneurs, risk takers, or trendsetters, we wouldn't have an innovative or progressive world. I, too, suffer from self-doubt sometimes, but I met a stranger who experiences like issues and we began to confide and uplift each other. We talked about how we were not doing well in our current profession; how the 9-5 lifestyle was not conducive to our full-time goal of starting a business. My thoughts at my desk* *range from my how I will sell my next cookie to what contents should be added or taken out of my baskets. My full time job is really my side hustle or silent investor, until my company becomes my full time check.*

○ ***WfW****: Women over forty, please don't be afraid of social media, embrace it! I have met women in their forties who feel defeated by younger women because they are more advanced with social media. Don't use it as a personal tool, but strictly for promoting and gaining a following for your company. Your online presence is just as potent as the physical one.*

Women in Power

Women are indeed powerful in the world of business, especially that of entrepreneurship. In 2008 Goldman Sachs launched its first ever *10,000 Women* business investment that would educationally prepare women for entrepreneurship via trainings and mentorship. The World Bank's International Finance Corporation (IFC) global finance facility created an initiative geared toward woman who owned small and medium sized enterprises. Amazingly, this program is a $600 million effort to enable 100,000 women-owned SME's to gain capital. Listen up ladies, tap into these funds to help create your business regardless of the size. In 2015 President Obama announced that he would be overseas and Private Investment Corporations would join Goldman Sachs' in financially equipping women in business. His goal is to generate 100,000 million dollars for new projects. Since launching, the program has reached over 25,000 women entrepreneurs. If your are serious about building your brand please look into this company and apply for the investments that you deserve. With Goldman Sachs, you are more competitive!

Multiple streams of income are required to become a millionaire. This is an idea to consider in determining when you endeavor to create wealth for yourself and leave a legacy for your family. Are you doing this as a side hustle because you enjoy it, or is it simply a means of extra cash? How big do you view your vision, how full is your glass? I set very high expectations for myself. Thus, when I developed my current business plan my initial vision was to create something different in terms of a traditional, restaurant style eatery. My vision was to have my mother assist me with an upscale, elegant, boutique style soul food restaurant. After pitching that idea to her and another family member, it failed before I could create the menu. My mother was grieving over the loss of my eldest brother and was not interested in any business. So I was advised to create something that I could shoulder alone. I thought to myself, I am a great sandwich maker, then an epiphany for Sassy Girl Sandwich & So. was born. Because of my talent to exquisitely present simple food creations and other accessories, I was driven to create a signature recipe for sandwiches. I also realized that I needed more products to reel in my audience as well as my income. I couldn't solely thrive off of my sandwich delivery service. Think about all of the successful companies that have multiple products: Apple, Wrigley, Mars, Subway, etc. I'm sure you either own or have shopped with one of these major corporations. After studying their recipe for attracting clients, I started to craft gift baskets that included cookies, personalized wine glasses, cups, and now I have started a new apparel line. Once you begin designing one product, the opportunities are endless! I will soon be able to add author and motivational speaker to my resume. When I'm out in the field or on a social media app, I express my vision to other woman who have a burning desire to create a business but don't know how to crack their DNA code. I inform them that their natural passion and past failures will create their profit. These two motives encouraged me to get on my soap box and start preaching and moving the crowd! We must break the chains of fear; actually it is to our benefit to concentrate on the word *fear* for a moment. It is a road block that's keeping people from starting their own business. Cracking Your DNA was written to unleash the fear of moving forward in becoming the business woman that you envision in your dreams but can't tangibly touch it. The stumbling block is fear of failure!

I want to speak to my forty-something and older women, who fear failure within social media. There's a reason Facebook calls your followers your friends, *it* is also your business friend. These are the most useful tools that will cost you little to nothing! Get with your children, grandchildren, nieces, etc to have them tutor you on how to grow your virtual following. These kids can teach you everything you need to know when it comes to utilizing and monetizing these tools. For example, if you don't know how to market your business these marketing/branding companies will do it for you at the click of a button! It's important that you know how to use buzz words because they drive people to your page. Don't be afraid to sell yourself through your bio on Instagram or through a status on Facebook. Always be prepared for an opportunity to share your one-minute elevator pitch, you never know who you'll cross paths with. Every person is a potential client if you can pitch well. I meet so many customers while I am out; I met my most recent customer at the checkout line in the grocery store in the middle of the night! I was preparing for a shower that requested a large amount of sandwiches so I wanted to have fresh veggies and meat. A gentleman in the line noticed that I had all of the materials a sandwich and commented, "Where's the cheese?" I said, "Oh, I have it already. You know your way around a sandwich!" We laughed and I informed him that make sandwiches for a living. He looked relived and replied, "Phew! My company is looking for someone to cater sandwiches for a party we're having this weekend!" I exclaimed, "I'm your lady!" I directed him to my website. He called me the next day to ask about my sandwich selections and quantities. I offered to bring him a few samples so that he could try them and share with his co-workers. He tried them and shortly after he called and placed an order with me. Preparation met opportunity and I met a new corporate client and check!

I recently meet a lady who offered services to take pictures, post and host your social media pages for a small fee. This was worth the investment if that task is too challenging for you. I personally enjoy managing my own pages, as it allows me the opportunity to be connect with my customers and learn which products are in demand and which should be retired. It provides me the motivation that I need to drive work ethic in building my building my brand. It's a personal gratification that I receive when people like my products, even more when I receive orders. This entire journey thus far has been one of overwhelming accomplishment. Cracking Your DNA is a part of my giving back, as I enjoy giving and sharing with as many women across the world as I can. This book will turn into a mentor or a coach, which could also enlighten you to start another stream of income. I believe that all things happen for a reason, I don't believe in accidental encounters, I believe that people are brought together for a reason, both in our personal and professional. The women that I have met on my journey have impacted my life and are helpful in my journey in entrepreneurship.

O **WfW**: *Follow the younger generation; they are for sure our future in terms of social media marketing for your services or goods. My sixteen year-old is my biggest adviser in terms of revising the current trends and marketing to people in her age group and older. My outlook on marketing strategies for my audience only brushes the surface when it comes an online presence. That's another reason for managing your own accounts, it gives you the opportunity to see what is trending. Most successful companies are doing just that and it's primarily because of the youth.*

O **WfW**: *Keep your presence consistent online as well as in person. This was my downfall; I would see businesses reposting their ads repeatedly and wonder why. It's because one may miss those customers that tune in at different times. Never go a day without* *posting something on your page even if you don't have anything new to share. Share an inspirational message, a picture from an event or anything relevant to your brand. This Word from Waddie comes from my teenager!*

○ **WfW**: *Utilize the "Live" tool that Facebook, and Instagram, recently added to their apps. I recently started using the Facebook live tool and initially it was scary but after a few practice sessions, I outgrew my fear and sharpened my professional speaking skills. My second major goal is to become articulate in my quest to become a public and motivational speaker. When I began this journey of becoming an author many years ago and was attempting to complete my first autobiography, I discovered that I wasn't as articulate as the others. Setting goals translates to being disciplined. This time I reached back to my practice of setting a goal for myself and stuck to writing and finishing this book. I didn't set a time table goal, but a number goal of writing 10,000 words. This advice came from an associate who is also an author. But I deiced to stick to my original word count goal, which was 6000 words a day! I assess my motivational level and am most creative when I have a multitude of topics roaming my mind. Mondays are my most busy writing days. I'm proud to say that I wrote this book in ten days.*

I only mention this as a way to show and demonstrate that whatever your goals are, you can achieve them if your minds chooses to do so.

O **WfW**: *Align yourself with others that share in your vision. Look into your state's requirements for licensing and tax requirement to start your business. Register your business name and patent your invention. Talk to a local banker about loans. I don't suggest you use your own money, but find an investor. Do as much research about starting a business as needed, network with others that have business and don't take someone else's experience and make it your experience. The success for you, is surely for you, and what you sow is what you'll reap. There are small businesses that offer business plan writing and business promoting at low-costs, take advantage of these pertinent skills. I'm using them to grow my business and build bridges with others. These are all services that I learned about via social media. My web designer is a young lady, who is awesome at her craft, and I have met tons of others whom I admire. I have so much respect for how our younger generation is hitting the World Wide Web to develop new ways to promote brands.*

O **WfW**: *The way in which we can touch customers globally is unfathomable to me sometimes. I have met and engaged with other woman who share my same vision. A business associate and I are virtual friends, as she resides in the UK and was running a promotion business on how to increase your Instagram following. My following skyrocketed 48hrs, I want from 84 followers to over 500! I was amazed and blown off of my feet! She and I struck up a long conversation regarding social media and how to generate followers. Since than I have picked up other tools to help me grow my online presence. My favorite quote is,* **"THE DREAM IS FREE/THE HUSTLE IS SOLD SEPARATELY!"** *Take this* *message with you on your journey of entrepreneurship, as we all need that daily motivational word to keep us going*

○ **WfW**: *My daily motivation isn't a message or phrase, it is what I visualize for my business. I have only one agenda, and that's to succeed and pass on experiences as I climb to the top.*

Acknowlededements

MY BROTHER, TONY GREEN 10-13-71 TO 07-09-15
who defeat the odds that the professional doctors had given my
mother, in regard to his illness. He was only supposed to live to
be 21 years-old, but when he left this earth he was 41years-old.
It gives me great joy and honor to know that he was a fighter
as well as a great survivor. He showed in his everyday life that
the limitations are the ones that you place on yourself. As a
child who was born with the inability to walk, run, jump, pick
himself up out of bed; he chose to enjoy the gift of life. He
displayed the characteristics of a great provider, family man and
father figure. Though he didn't bear children of his own, he
constantly mentored many youth. He never succumbed to street
violence, nor was he ever recruited into gangs. Tony could give
you advice on all sorts of things as he walked and experienced
life. He mentors my son who desires to become a great athlete,
and although he himself never bounced a ball nor kicked a
football, he could provide the ultimate tool to get become
successful. I guess in a way he lived through those who could

do the things that he knew he would never ever experience. He took the life that God had given him and made it the best one could imagine. There is no better role mode than Tony Green. He was a man who pursued his dreams of becoming a rapper/ entertainer, author, and even an entrepreneur. He cracked his DNA early in life. I took his advice to start a business and he was right there directing me toward then right people who could help me become self-reliant. I dive right in and wait to see the results of my actions, which work for me, and which are not profitable. By having the support of my brother (mentor) mother (supporter), who have both uplifted me with their words, I know that I am moving upward in my quest to success, and so are you. As I conclude my Words from Waddie and personal experiences on my journey of starting and growing a business, I hope that you will share it will another person that needs that guidance and development in cracking their DNA. This book is apart of my legacy, not only for me but for my future generations. My goal is to use my DNA to create scholarship programs that foster young entrepreneurship. Recycle this book by passing it on to someone else that may need some direction on how to map out their DNA.

O **WfW**: *Write out your vision, as it is more realistic when you can see it on paper.*

The only thing that stand between you and success is starting on it! Keep in mind that entrepreneur is a lifestyle! You determine how you'll fuel that lifestyle with unleaded, mid-grade or premium fuel to get you where you'd like to go. Don't be afraid to put a stranger on that same road, as he or she may be that element you need to help you along the way. Your path to success is your ability to network which will lead to your net worth! I ask that you incorporate prayers into your daily agenda when it comes to pursuing your goal of entrepreneurship, judge your accomplishments by all the things you had to endure in order to arrive success.

Your distinct, natural abilities are characteristics of becoming an effective entrepreneur. You have to possess action oriented traits, and graduate from failure without regret. I practice this and it's highly effective toward keeping your business presently on the mind of current and potential customers. Be fearless where others are stagnant. ADHD, from a professional standpoint, can be a serious disorder and should be treated. However, when I refer to this disorder I speak to only certain symptoms, not the entire disorder. Overly hyper, eager about your next business venture and other adrenaline rushes that entrepreneurs experience are all great feelings, but are akin to ADHD.

The **bounce back** affect is simple, when you fall, spring up and keep it moving, in that order. I totally can relate to this scenario. As I closed my salon, in less than five days I was back at my next business.

The **crafty** affect; I am the Puffy Combs of crafting. Where others see nothing, I see gold. I use to refer to myself as the next Black Martha Stewart. I admire how she would take other ideas and make them her own and capitalize in the process. I still strive to become a house hold name in the crafting industry. I'm a thrift store, garage picker guru. My house is full of thrift store re-dos and craigslist finds. I pride myself in making things beautiful, so much that my cousin suggested I make that my slogan from it. I recently watched an interview with Kim Kardashian, where she was asked about how she created her 100 million dollar empire on simple, everyday life events. She said that it takes some kind of talent. There's a reality show called "The Real Hustler", where women who have been to jail are studied for their success. These woman were from all over the U.S. and were entrepreneurs. I mentioned this to a group chat online and suggests that we should pitch our own reality show to prove that we were the *true* Divas of hustle. The moral of this true life experience is that all women entrepreneurs truly share the same vision, but need to network and share ideas on how to join forces to collectively achieve a common goal. Some successful opportunities can literally be at your fingertips. Leave your comfort zone! Become a multifunctional innovator.

Finally, some key components in cracking your DNA are being transparent, goal oriented, open for receiving advice from relevant people, education, become as resourceful as you can, follow your dreams, receive failure, share, network, recycle, engage, keep going! These are all characteristics that are currently apart of you and that really should come as natural as your distinct abilities. The success stories I read about show how many entrepreneurs have been knocked down and someone reading this book may know of someone that has experienced such entrepreneurial pain. Be determined by failure, not defeated. I have practiced this several times in life. I'm the woman that has tried everything from home daycare, cleaning service, real estate investor, landlord, salon owner and now professional sandwich maker! You will find your niche if you don't give up on yourself after every little or big failure. That's the main reason you need a mentor, coach or engage into some type of social group that share in your vision. Hello, and thank you, to the many successful people that pick up this book!

www.ingramcontent.com/pod-product-compliance
Lightning Source LLC
Chambersburg PA
CBHW021048180526
45163CB00005B/2336